SC
N

GW00836346

Neil M. Gunn's

The Silver Darlings

John Burns

Association for Scottish Literary Studies 2014

Published by
Association for Scottish Literary Studies
Scottish Literature
7 University Gardens
University of Glasgow
Glasgow G12 8QH
www.asls.org.uk

ASLS is a registered charity no. SC006535

First published 2014

A CIP catalogue for this title
is available from the British Library

ISBN 978-1-906841-18-8

The Association for Scottish Literary Studies
acknowledges the support of Creative Scotland
towards the publication of this book.

ALBA | CHRUTHACHAIL

CONTENTS

SCOTNOTES

Study guides to major Scottish writers and literary texts

Produced by the Education Committee
of the Association for Scottish Literary Studies

the route of the river of his childhood back to its source. The journey is also a journey to discover the roots of his own nature through exploring his own character, his relationship with his parents, and his understanding of the community in which he had grown up. In this book Gunn's extraordinary prose takes the reader close in to the rhythm and movement of Kenn's thought processes.

During World War II when, despite the horror around them, people actually read a great deal, Gunn produced several important books as well as *The Silver Darlings*. These included the philosophical *The Serpent* (1943) in which an old man regarded as the village atheist looks back over his life in search of understanding and enlightenment. *Young Art and Old Hector* (1942), a collection of stories about the adventures and escapades of a young boy and an old man in a Highland village, is a book about the getting of wisdom as the boy learns much from the old man. These heart-warming stories were criticised by Naomi Mitchison, who accused Gunn of escapism because he had not dealt with the dark realities of the war directly. His response was to write *The Green Isle of the Great Deep* (1944), a dystopian novel in which he placed the same boy and the same old man in a dark and disturbing totalitarian landscape to test them. It is a novel which bears comparison with George Orwell's *Nineteen Eighty-Four* (1948) as J. B. Pick pointed out in an article exploring both writers' attempts to face the horror of life during and just after the war. Several later novels followed, in which the dark shadow of war serves as a backdrop as Gunn explored ways in which humanity might salvage dignity and survive in a world that is full of threat and violence.

For Gunn, one of the strongest sources of the resilient strength needed to survive lay in the community in which he had grown up. Some saw this as part of a naïve belief in a "golden age", but not only did Gunn believe that he had grown up in a community that looked after all of its members, he could describe it from his own experience. As a writer of striking intelligence – T. S. Eliot said Gunn had the "finest analytical mind he had encountered"[2] – Gunn had also commented publicly in the press on economics and politics as well as serving on various commissions concerned with improving and developing the Highlands as a region. He understood very well how people lived in Highland communities.

His firm belief was that to deal with the darkness of contemporary life, man had to face it with the light of personal and communal wisdom. Some saw this as wilful escapism, especially in the 1950s when he declared an interest in Zen Buddhism. Yet as F. R. Hart has pointed out, when Gunn discovered Zen it "was less the discovery of something new than the delighted recognition, in a remote place, of something he had known and sought to convey all along".[3] To many in Britain at that time, Zen seemed completely alien yet in America writers like Jack Kerouac, Gary Snyder and Allen Ginsberg were beginning to use it at the cutting edge of contemporary fiction and poetry. Gunn's own interest in Zen was concerned with its attempt to make us appreciate the extraordinary nature of our ordinary existence.

Gunn essentially retired from writing in the 1950s after producing a searching study of how to deal with violence in the novel *Bloodhunt* (1952), a novel about a man's quest for "goodness" in the modern world, *The Well at the World's End* (1951), and a bold foray into the unknown in *The Other Landscape* (1954). After that came the final book, *The Atom of Delight* (1956) in which he used his personal experience to explore and describe his lifelong quest for insight. It is a book that puzzled many of his contemporaries, but it has inspired and enthused many younger Scottish writers, like the novelist and short-story writer Alan Spence, and the playwrights Tom McGrath and John McGrath.

Neil Gunn died in January 1973.

Notes

1. The reality of course was more complex, and recent scholarship has shown that the "Kailyard" label itself is a stereotype that has possibly outlived its usefulness, as later nineteenth century Scotland did in fact produce a great deal of important and thought-provoking literature.
2. *A Highland Life*, p. 138.
3. *Neil M. Gunn: The Man and the Writer*, p. 53.

2. INTRODUCTION TO
THE SILVER DARLINGS

The Silver Darlings was published in 1941. Set in Caithness, in the early nineteenth century, in the aftermath of the Highland Clearances, the book describes how people, removed from the land, have to learn a new way of life living by the sea. This is very difficult and the book describes how newly-married Catrine MacHamish loses her young husband, Tormad, to a Royal Navy press-gang on his first attempt at fishing the sea. Catrine moves to Dale (the modern Helmsdale) where she gives birth to her son, Finn.

In Dale, the people are more advanced in their knowledge of the sea and are participating in the rise of the herring fishing industry, one of the most economically successful industries in nineteenth-century Scotland. It gives work to fishermen, gutters, curers, boat-builders and many others. The story of Finn's personal growth is echoed in the economic growth of the community.

Catrine is attracted to Roddie Sinclair, a very successful skipper, and the book follows the tangled relationships between Catrine, Finn and Roddie until, in the end, Catrine and Roddie marry. This disturbs Finn, and the uneasy situation only becomes resolved when Finn falls in love with the girl Una. The book ends on the eve of their wedding.

3. INTERPRETATIVE CHAPTER SUMMARIES

Chapter I: The Derelict Boat

The book opens with a young man called Tormad getting ready to set off on his first attempt at fishing on the sea. He is newly married and his wife, Catrine, does not want him to go. The sea had already killed Catrine's uncle so, despite her pride in Tormad's bravery, she is against him going to sea.

As he prepares to set off she tries to stop him in a scene in which Gunn quickly sketches in the nature of their relationship. Newly married, they are shy and tentative with each other, trying out their new roles of man and wife, just beginning to learn how to make their relationship work. Their love for each other is fierce and physically intense. The vehemence of Catrine's attempts to stop him from going to sea are shocking and, in a culture that values emotional restraint, embarrassing. When Tormad leaves he is shaken, as such a display of emotion has revealed a side of his wife he had not seen before. Only when Catrine appears on the shore to see him off does he regain his equilibrium as this is a sign that she has realised he has no option but to go for the good of others. Throughout the book Gunn moves back and forth between the lives of individuals and the lives of a whole community. He is describing a society where the individual is an active and valued part of a whole culture.

The sea is a huge brooding presence in the book. It is the unknown that everyone must face. It underlies all the human relationships in the book. In its implacable mystery and unknowability it is the standard against which we must judge the growth of the human characters. When Tormad and his crew have put to sea they are awed by the sea's immensity:

> They had never before been so far from land, and the slow movement of the sea became a living motion under them. It brimmed up against the boat and choked its own mouth, then moved away; and came again and moved away, without end, slow, heedless, and terrible, its power restrained, like

to Tormad's disappearance and her decision to leave Helmsdale to go and live with an old friend, Kirsty MacKay, in Dunster (the modern Dunbeath), a small village further up the coast.

Catrine had once had a dream in which she and Tormad were standing by a pool or loch near a wood, "heavy with clustered [rowan] berries of a menacing blood-red" (p. 35). A black horse came from the wood. Tormad mounted and rode into the water to his certain death. This dream had stayed with her, "and probably it was the strongest element behind her fierce irrational clinging to him before he had left their home to go to sea in his black boat" (p. 37). In referring to the dream and to the folk motif of the kelpie, the water spirit that lures men to their deaths, Gunn is pointing to the role the unconscious plays in our lives, an area of human psychology that had recently been opened up for discussion by Freud and Jung. More specifically he is using materials from Celtic myths that would be well-known to Catrine and to those around her at that time.

This dream, and another described on pp. 43–44, convince her that Tormad is dead which conflicts with the view of the community that he is probably still alive and now serving in the Navy. This causes a problem with regard to her status in the community. She knows she is a widow, but in the eyes of others she is still a married woman. In a community that, despite the changes it is going through, tends to uphold traditional patterns of behaviour, this makes her something of a non-person, as she is unable fully to take on one social role or the other.

On the other hand, these chapters show us a great deal about Catrine's sense of herself, and give a clear indication of her independence and strength of character. At first (pp. 38–39) she is utterly devastated by the news of Tormad's disappearance, and is barely in control of her actions but keeps going "blindly". This "dry, barren state" gradually gives way to one which is "grave and calm" (p. 44) as she begins to take control of her emotions and decides to move away from the "dumb misery" (p. 44) of living in Helmsdale. Like Chris Guthrie in Lewis Grassic Gibbon's *Sunset Song*, who confounds her community's expectations by running the family croft on her own after her father's death, Catrine makes her own decision about what is best for her. In their different ways, both women show their independence and individuality. Catrine's mother is "appalled" when Catrine says she will give away the croft and Tormad's share of his boat, because, her mother says, it is not hers to give, but belongs to "her man" (p. 45). Having shown how "everything that spoke of power and wealth had to be feared" (p. 27) in relation to the government, the Navy and the press-gang, here Gunn shows how such issues operate even within the intimacy of marriage. His view of the Gaelic culture he so admires is not naïve. He is fully aware that this community has its own complexities.

Chapter III: Catrine Goes Into A Strange Country
In Chapter III the second of the book's momentous journeys occurs as Catrine walks "over the Ord" from Sutherland into Caithness, Gunn's own country. The journey is long and hard and she becomes like a Biblical character or one of Thomas Hardy's characters, journeying alone through a landscape that is disturbing because new and unknown. Like Tormad's own journey it is physically and psychologically difficult. At one point (p. 49) we see her poised on the cliff road between the moorland and the sea acutely aware of the dangers that could lie in either, although her instinct is always to hold to the landward side. Many years later, Gunn will write about himself:

> As his existence had two parents, so it had the earth and the sea. If his mother was the earth, his father was the sea. (*The Atom of Delight*, p. 101)

Again we can see that, for all its surface realism, the book works on many levels simultaneously.

Echoes of Tormad's nervous encounters with the unknown are evident in the passing of a stagecoach, which Catrine cannot afford to take, and which signifies to her "the traffic and pomp of the great world, its ruthless power and speed, its cities and its wealth" (p. 51–52). She is frightened too by the Scots speech of the Lowland shepherd she encounters.

(For many modern readers it is a shock to be constantly reminded that most of the main characters in this book speak Gaelic, because most Scots now speak Scottish English and Gaelic and Scots are used less and less.)

Near the end of her journey Catrine meets Roddie Sinclair who shows her the way to Kirsty's house. Roddie is almost an ideal version of the man Tormad might have grown into. At twenty-five, he has the natural assurance that comes from traffic with the sea. For Gunn, whose father was the captain of a fishing boat, the fisherman is a symbol of balance and integrity. The sea is Roddie's natural element. He is a successful skipper because he respects but does not fear its mystery and power. Everything he does in this first meeting puts Catrine at her ease and Gunn hints right away at the fact that she is attracted to him physically. It is there in the way she notes the way he moves, the way he is built, the way he unobtrusively changes the subject when he realises he has said something that causes pain or embarrassment. We have to remember that despite the barren state of mind caused by the loss of her husband she is pregnant with his son. Her mind is at once numb yet intensely raw and alive. Indeed, the many references to Catrine's closeness to the natural world in this chapter highlight her sensual nature.

It is with Roddie that she first sees the House of Peace, the ruins of an old Celtic monastery, that will be so important in the life of her son, Finn, later in the book. She repeats its name "in a tone of soft wonder" (p. 61) and it is "like a benediction [sounding] softly in her mind". This is the first moment of peace she has felt since losing Tormad.

Still in a slightly dazed state of mind, she reaches Kirsty's croft in Dunster and Gunn introduces two of the book's most important minor characters: Kirsty and her father. Kirsty's straightforward anger at what has happened is a real tonic to Catrine (p. 64). So is her practicality as she feeds Catrine and gives her a place to sleep after her long journey. Before bed, Kirsty's father reads from the Gaelic Bible as was the custom in Highland houses at that time. Despite his age and failing memory he is kind and gracious in his speech. When he reads from the Bible he inadvertently chooses the twenty-

third chapter of the book of Psalms, the very passage Tormad
had chosen when the newly-married couple had read the Bible
themselves for the first time in their own house. Catrine's
memory of that time is of its quiet shy intimacy and, although
a minor incident in the book, it pulses almost unbearably with
the intensity of her love for the husband she has lost.

She is greatly moved by the old man's reading and by his
demeanour:

> [...] his eyes clear open and yet faintly veiled, almost as if
> he were looking at her from a distance with the unearthly
> calm and consideration there might be in the eyes of God.
> (p. 69)

That "consideration" points to an attitude that is respectful
(considerate) of the reality of the lives of others. It stands in
stark opposition to the attitude of those who ordered and
carried out the Clearances, and those who sent the press-gangs
to take men for the Navy.

Chapter IV: The First Hunt For The Silver Darlings
Chapter IV moves two years back in time and shows how
"Special" Hendry, a local publican and businessman in Dunster,
had set Roddie up as the skipper of one of his boats. The
chapter suggests something of the excitement of the birth of
the new industry of herring fishing, something that will help
people survive and will bring wealth and prosperity after the
horror of the Clearances, especially after the government
increased the bounty on every cran of herring landed.

It is an important chapter because it contrasts the "energetic
and business-like" (p. 70) Hendry with the shy young fisherman who is "slightly embarrassed" (p. 73) at all this talk of
money. The two men represent two ways of looking at the
world: the one modern, entrepreneurial and go-ahead; the
other traditional, canny and conservative. At first glance this
might seem like another example of money and power exploit-
ing those who have no head for such things, but Gunn is at
pains to make Special a likeable, lively, entertaining character
and he also shows Roddie to be a capable-enough business-

man when he works out the terms for ownership of the boat. Neither man is naïve, and both understand fully the nature of the deal they have made. There is nothing wrong with business and economic initiative Gunn seems to be saying, as long as it does not overreach itself.

Hendry's vision is that of the hard-headed businessman:

> "Don't you see that the sea in front of our doors is going to be a gold-mine? That we are now at the beginning of what will mean fortunes for those who know how to take advantage of it? The news is running along the coasts like wild-fire." (p. 72)

Hendry's vision and drive will make money for himself, and also give a great boost to the community and help fuel the need for fishermen, boat-builders, net-makers, creel-makers and gutters. It also necessitates more contact with a world beyond their isolated villages, as curers and fishermen "with Scots tongues that few could understand, turned the foreshore into Babel in the first week of July" (p. 82).

Roddie, who already has a natural affinity with the sea, has access to a support system that will allow him to develop his skills in a way that will benefit himself and his whole community. This simple fact throws into stark relief the bravery of Tormad and his crew setting out on their first fateful voyage with very little knowledge of the sea.

The chapter ends by giving the reader a first taste of the excitement of the times when Roddie's first attempts to catch herring in his new boat are unsuccessful and a feeling of despondency settles over the fleet. Then, standing on the quayside, Hendry sees the *Morning Star* approaching:

> But when, at long last, the *Morning Star* was seen coming round the Head, low to the sea, as if nearly sunk, Mr Hendry stood dead still. A voice cried, "By the Lord, he's in them to the gunnels!" (pp. 83–84)

In a brief coda to this chapter the words of two old men again underline the sharp contrast between this vibrant new world and the cannier old world in which they had grown up. They describe Roddie in religious terms as one who has come to save them, while at the same time they regard this new-found wealth as "hardly right" (p. 85).

Chapter V: Finn And The Butterfly

In Chapters V, VI and VII, the focus shifts away from Catrine and Roddie, on to her son Finn. They show Finn beginning to grow up and become aware of himself as a person in his own right and separate from his mother. They also show how hard it is for her to accept this.

In Chapter V we see Finn at four and a half, chasing a butterfly away from his home so that he ends up far away, excited by his new-found freedom, but also rather disturbed by it. This ambivalence, which is an essential insight in Gunn's fiction, becomes particularly acute when he finally catches up with a butterfly and kills it. In one shattering moment he sees that beauty is fragile and easily destroyed. He also realises that he is capable of terrible violence. It is a lesson we all learn, a rite of passage that is often the subject of literature, but Gunn makes it new by the way his description of the incident comes from Finn's point of view. He draws us in to the expanding and exciting world Finn encounters so that when he kills the butterfly we feel the terrible shock of recognition. The whole episode is told like a self-contained short story and has within it strong elements of the fable or the parable. When he panics and runs away distraught at the realisation of what he has done, Roddie finds him exhausted at the House of Peace and is on the point of persuading him to return home when Catrine comes looking for him in a very agitated state. Several things coalesce here: Catrine is panic-stricken at the loss of Finn which reminds her of the disappearance of his father, Tormad, taken by the sea; we see Catrine, Finn and Roddie almost like a family group at the House of Peace where she and Roddie had rested on the day he led her to Kirsty's house; Finn, in beginning to grow away from his mother, is drawn to Roddie and his world, the world of those who go to sea.

Near the end of the chapter as she comforts Finn, we catch a glimpse of the intensity of a mother's love in a way that echoes her own mother's feelings towards her at the end of Chapter II:

> Though Catrine might have killed many butterflies to save him a scratch, she found herself without words. She caressed his back, and stared over his head at the intermingling of terrors and meanings in life, hidden, but there. Her lips trembled. The meanings had started to take her son away from her. Already the terrible knowledge of good and evil was in him. He had killed the butterfly. (pp. 99–100)

In what is essentially Finn's chapter, Gunn focuses clearly on Catrine's thoughts and feelings.

The chapter ends with Roddie visiting Catrine, to see if she wants him to take any messages back to Helmsdale as he is going there in the morning, but the focus shifts again as Gunn lets us hear the rather awkward conversation of two people who are attracted to each other but who, for various reasons, can barely admit it even to themselves. He conveys this by the mixture of humour and genuine concern, the teasing and the awkward, short sentences, the lengthening of a conversation that does not need to be prolonged.

Chapter VI: The Land And The Sea
As well as allowing Gunn, through Kirsty, to present some of the history of the Clearances and the resulting diaspora, with many Highlanders becoming explorers, traders, fighters, and more worryingly, colonisers, he also shows us something of the domestic reality of the lives of the people. We see Catrine, Finn and Kirsty having to avert a disaster as the cow Bel gets into the corn. The incident is presented with humour but in their straitened economic circumstances, the loss of the corn would be a real blow to them. The scene is almost medieval, or like something in a folk-tale or fairytale, as surrounded by hens and other animals they try to coax and cajole the cow back to her own territory.

The liveliness is undercut, though, by Kirsty telling Catrine that she is over-protective of Finn –

"You're coddling that boy too much" (p. 106)

– and by a glimpse of Catrine on her own imagining the men, including Roddie, at sea as a storm is getting up and fearing for their lives:

Her hatred of the sea had gone deep as an instinct. (p. 118).

The danger of life at sea is highlighted as well when Roddie's boat is feared lost in the storm and Hendry drives his gig along the coast to discover what has happened (because, although he does care for Roddie, the boat means money to him, and Roddie is a kind of talisman for the continuing success of his business). Roddie and his crew are found safe but exhausted and the conversation between Hendry and Roddie shows that for all his genuine concern, the landsman has no real conception of just how hard and dangerous life at sea really is.

Chapter VII: Finn Blows His Trumpet
In a brief scene at the beginning of this chapter Roddie answers a question about whether or not he will marry by saying simply,

"I have married the sea." (p. 133)

This is taken as a confirmation of his commitment to his boat and his work as a fisherman, but it also stems from the fact that he and Catrine, for all the attraction between them cannot allow this to develop into anything more as, in the eyes of the community, Catrine is still married to Tormad, although at a very deep level she knows he is dead.

They are brought together again at the time of the November hill market, one of the most important community events of the year. At nearly five years old this is the first time Finn has gone to the market and he is almost overwhelmed by it:

> He forgot his mother [...] His mind could not take in the
> scene, for the upward slope, far as the eye could see, was a
> mass of human beings. Bellowing cattle, bleating sheep,
> barking dogs, a continuous uproar of voices; and the whole
> hillside moving. It was incredible and terrifying. (p. 135)

Having lived quietly in a small house with only his mother
and Kirsty for company, he is suddenly thrust into this great
world of noise and movement and colour. Roddie takes him
round the market while Catrine is busy trying to sell her cow,
and buys him a toy trumpet. Gunn describes accurately Finn's
pride and excitement in receiving this gift. He also makes us
feel acutely the boy's distress when, having plucked up the
courage to blow it, he cannot make a sound (p. 139). Like
Charles Dickens or James Joyce, Gunn is masterly when
describing the intensity of a child's world, all the hopes and
fears which a small child feels with the kind of searing intensity most adults have long left behind. Roddie kneels down
beside him and, with all the tenderness of a father, shows him
how to do it in a way that is simple and kind and does not
make him feel silly or inadequate. It is a very small but very
telling moment.

The chapter is full of the life and gaiety of the market, a
subject that echoes through Scottish literature from the
medieval "Peblis to the Play", through Fergusson and Burns
to George Mackay Brown. Perhaps, in the light of the next
chapter, it also has in it elements of John Bunyan's description of Vanity Fair in *The Pilgrim's Progress*, and of the
Victorian novelist William Makepeace Thackeray's *Vanity
Fair*. Gunn also describes sensitively Finn's shyness among
the men who show him much kindness yet also gently tease
him as if starting to accept him as one of their own. We have
to remember that, as Gunn previously described in *Butcher's
Broom*, such a society as this had sharp divisions between the
world of the men and the world of the women.

The mood changes sharply when, tired out after the excitement of the day, Finn chats to Catrine about all he had seen.
It is a pleasant end to the day, but the mood changes when
he says he wants to go to sea like Roddie when he grows up:

"Mama does not want you to go to sea. You must never go to
sea. Do you hear? Never."

"Why?" He was astonished at her vehemence.

"Because I don't want you to. Because people who go to
sea get drowned. The sea is an angry cruel place. You must
promise me never to go to sea." (p. 144)

We can feel and understand Catrine's fear, but we also realise
that in revealing this fear to Finn she is being unfair. However
we read it, it highlights the tangle of emotions that binds Finn,
Catrine and Roddie together.

Chapter VIII: The Spirit And The Flesh

Chapter VIII begins by describing the way Sandy Ware, the
Catechist, goes about his business, and gives some insight
into the power of Christianity in the community. It might also
suggest that the learning of the Catechism by rote was not a
particularly spiritual experience. There is more to the getting
of wisdom than learning off by heart a half-understood arrange-
ment of finely expressed words.

The chapter also describes, in flashback, the death of Kirsty's
father and the birth of Finn himself. On his deathbed the old
man seems to have nothing left in him but kindness and tells
Catrine that she and Finn are to have his house if Kirsty dies.
His carefully chosen words have great authority and power
because he knows he is about to die:

"[...] somehow you have brought peace to my last days. I
want to thank you, Catrine; for my time has come upon me."
(p. 155)

This is a spirituality that is genuine and moving. Minutes
later he is dead and Finn is born in the byre. Life and death
are close companions and for people in that place and at that
time, as for most people through the ages, life was lived close
to their animals.

We also see Catrine receive a letter from Ronnie, one of the
men press-ganged with Tormad, telling the people back home
that they are all well enough. He does not mention Tormad

which leads Catrine to think that perhaps an earlier letter
had gone astray, a letter that had explained how he had died.
The fact that the letter had been written *for* Ronnie reminds
us that literacy was still not all that common in early nineteenth century Scotland. It also reminds a modern audience
of the difficulty of communication in a world before email,
texting and mobile telephones.

The chapter ends with Finn dreaming that he had blown
his trumpet with such force that, like Joshua at Jericho,
he had brought the walls of the House of Peace tumbling
down. The dream is so vivid that the next day he has to
check that the walls are still there. He does this nonchalantly
but his very nonchalance suggests that, like Catrine, he is
troubled by the way dreams and reality seem to be so closely
intertwined.

Chapter IX: The Seashore

Finn, now thirteen, and his friend Donnie are at the harbour
enjoying the bustle and banter of the fishermen and the gutters,
the sheer life of the place. Finn is obviously well-known by
everyone and we get the sense that this is something the boys
have done before, although he had to lie to Kirsty to get away
from the croft. Gunn presents a lively picture of the scene:

> Fishermen were already spreading their nets on the outskirts
> of the gutting stations, one net overlapping another, so that
> each drift was a long, rectangular darkness upon the green
> grass of river flat or sloping brae. [...] barefooted men walking
> smartly in a line [...] an enormous number of herring in the
> wooden gutting boxes [...] rows of women, their heads bobbing
> up and down as they stooped, caught a herring, gutted it,
> and flung it into a basket [...] their hands working so quickly
> that you couldn't see exactly what the blade of the knife did.
> (p. 163)

It is a picture of people hard at work, but for the boys the
harbour represents excitement, freedom from their parents,
and an acceptance of them by the rest of the community as
individuals.

The excitement continues when they go a little further, to a sloping skerry which Finn knows is a good place to fish. They become so involved in this, especially in attempting to land an eel that puts up a real fight, that they do not notice the sea slowly surrounding them so that they are almost cut off from the shore. This is when Roddie and Catrine discover them. Guilt-ridden, and embarrassed at his stupidity in being caught out by the movement of the sea, Finn is at the same time determined to land the eel before making it safely back to shore. The sensible thing to do would be to forget the eel and get back on shore but we can see clearly the two opposing impulses working in the boy who wants to show that he is no longer a child but a capable young man. When he reaches the shore he is gruff and off-hand with Catrine and with Roddie, as if he is fully in command of the situation and cannot see what all the fuss is about. Roddie seems to accept this as a normal response. Catrine, though, is "[...] so angry that for a moment she could not speak" (p. 168). Her fear of the sea and her son's love of it has driven a bitter wedge between them. From this point on their relationship will never be the same. She will have to face the fact that her son really is growing up and does not need her in the same way that he did when he was younger. It is a difficult lesson for her to learn, but it is a lesson all parents have to learn. Hopefully they also learn to accept the reality of their child's new life. The child, too, needs to learn acceptance of the parent.

Kirsty sees them with shrewd amusement on their separate returns, and observes that, in Finn,

The man was stirring! (p. 170)

This feeling of growing maturity is very soon put to the test.

At the celebration for the ending of the harvest, Finn, proud of his involvement in the man's world, misses Roddie in the house and goes outside to talk to him. Just inside the byre door he comes upon Roddie and Catrine:

[...] her face white and scared and Roddie, a yard from her, silent. They looked at him but did not speak, and in that

> queer, still moment Finn's breast seemed to crush together
> and fall down inside him. (p. 176)

The sight shocks him to the core:

> Roddie and his mother.
>   He had never dreamt of anything between them. He knew
> all about flesh relations. He could not think [...]
>   Roddie was thirty-eight and Catrine thirty-three. In Finn's
> thought they were fixed in their courses like the sun and the
> moon. They were old people. [...]
>   Suddenly he hated what he had seen, hated it in dumb,
> frightened anger, hated its bodily crush, its tragic pallor,
> and moved swiftly on to the moor, as if the ghost of his father
> had come up behind him. (p. 177)

The novel's three characters are here held in a suspension of
awareness. Roddie and Catrine are apprehensive about Finn's
reaction to their relationship while, for Finn himself, on the
verge of manhood, restless and troubled by his own body, this
incident opens up before him a great chasm of uncertainty
and confusion. Uncertain enough about his own developing
identity, he sees that Roddie and Catrine, the two fixed poles
in relation to which he is trying to define his own personality,
are also capable of change. This whole complex of feelings is
too much for Finn who rebels against it and shuts off his mind
with anger and bitterness, turning away from Roddie and
Catrine and more and more in on himself:

> After that night Finn cunningly hid things inside himself,
> yet at the same time found a greater release in life. (p. 177)

Chapter X: The Coming Of The Plague

Chapters X to XIII mark another important stage in Finn's
growing up, and bring Roddie and Catrine closer, although
this very closeness brings with it increasing tensions.
    The plague, which Gunn points out is really cholera, comes
insidiously to Dunster, but its effects are shocking in the
intensity with which it grips people and the speed with which

it kills them. Death from cholera is a disgusting and terrible experience physically and mentally because the sufferer probably knows they have already passed it on to other family members or friends. Those same family members or friends are torn between caring for the dying, or leaving them to die alone in the hope that they might protect themselves. Because of the virulence of the disease this dilemma is particularly acute in such a close-knit community.

The reader feels this with increasing horror when s/he reads how a young fisherman visiting his mother-in-law realises that he has entered the house of a woman dying of cholera. His sister-in-law is distraught and tells him that her mother had driven the family out so that they might be saved. Gunn describes the horror, the "slime" (p. 196), the "sour, diarrhœtic smell" (p. 195) that clings to his throat, the shock in his own body when he realises that he might die. Not only will he have to tell his wife of her mother's death, he might have the disease himself and might pass it on to his wife. That is what happens and Gunn describes the increasing hopelessness, the fear and anger the young man feels, in such a way that it is almost a relief when death takes them. The young couple remind us of Catrine and Tormad, and their situation prepares us for the moment when Catrine herself falls prey to the disease.

People are very frightened, because in the early nineteenth century no-one really understood the nature of the disease or how to deal with it. Sandy Ware, the Catechist, even says that it is "God's judgement" on the people for enjoying the financial rewards that were beginning to come from the herring fishing (p. 193).

Shortly after the death of the young fisherman and his wife, Kirsty asks Finn to go to Dale to visit relatives. She is really trying to send him away so that he will be safe if the disease spreads, but it is a while before he realises this. On his walk to Dale he becomes aware that people do not want to be close to him, and realises from the questions they ask,

> [...] that the folk in and around Helmsdale believed the plague was so virulent in Dunster that houses were being burned every day

to destroy the taint of the disease and to prevent it spreading (p. 205). Despite his granny's pleading he cuts short his visit so that he can return home. When he does he meets Roddie. Something in his short journey has changed him:

> Finn felt grown-up and so free from awkwardness that when Roddie told him of two more cases of the plague he felt grave and responsible. (p. 207)

This new maturity is challenged when Roddie tells him that Kirsty is ill. Whatever feelings of panic and fear Finn might feel at this news they are kept in check by Roddie's quiet, "reflective" (p. 208), reasonable tone. When he goes to speak to his mother across the burn Roddie's "cool, responsible tone" (p. 211) stayed with him and gave him strength. Catrine, too, gives him strength by her refusal to panic or to show fear. Yet when he leaves her to stay for the night at Roddie's house his mind is "desolate" (p. 212):

> He had no desire for Roddie's company now [...] The only thing that was near him [...] was his mother's voice; and not only because it was her voice, but because it was the voice of courage in her warm, kind body.
> In these moments there was no resentment against her, only a far understanding, beyond which there was nothing. (p. 212)

Here the abstract thought linked to the sensual image of Catrine's "warm, kind body" reminds us that in a sense Finn and Roddie each want Catrine for their own.

Unable to go directly to Roddie's, Finn stops at the House of Peace where he falls asleep and dreams of the figure of an old monk who does not speak but simply looks at him and smiles. Like his mother Finn seems to be susceptible to such moments. Like his mother, he finds in these "'lost' moment[s] of awakening" (p. 213) a meaning that goes beyond words:

> [...] the look was extraordinarily full of understanding, and somewhere in it there was a faint humour [...] [The smile]

knew all about Finn, and told him nothing – not out of
compassion, but out of needlessness. (p. 214)

This encounter steadies him, which says a great deal about
his maturity and courage. The "ease and comfort" (p. 214)
gifted by the vision helps him to cope with the difficult situation he is in. The vision stays with him as he tries to sleep in
Roddie's house later. But another strange encounter happens
there when, almost asleep, he witnesses Roddie and his crew
putting out the fire. This strange episode tests his nerve "for
no fire was ever put out from one year's end to the other" (pp.
216–17). He feels as if he is watching "some dreadful, unim-
aginable rite". With some difficulty Rob starts a new fire which
it is hoped will bring new hope to the village. It is an ancient
rite of cleansing. Water boiled over the new fire is carefully
sprinkled around to bless the house. Even the animals in the
byre are blessed.

The blessing is not immediate in its effect. Next day Finn
discovers that Kirsty's illness is indeed the plague. Meeting
Catrine outside the cottage, at "the door of death" (p. 225),
Finn is again "desolate". Roddie is the one who goes closest to
her, the one who speaks to her while Finn waits "empty and
forlorn" (p. 225). He decides to go in search of the new doctor
he has heard about while Roddie goes for help to a traditional
healer, Hector Bethune, probably named after the famous
Beaton family of healers. Finn sets off to walk twenty miles
in the dark of night to find the doctor.

Chapter XI: Catrine And Kirsty
Catrine cares for the dying Kirsty in the close confinement of
the cottage. Because of Kirsty's kindness to her and to Finn
she cannot leave her to die alone, even if it means she is putting
herself in extreme danger. Naturally the situation makes her
look back over her life and sheer exhaustion makes many of
her memories seem very real. When she thinks of Tormad it
is as if he is still very much present to her:

She felt him with her hands, her fingers going through his
hair, sometimes gripping it and hanging on until he yelled

and threatened her and they rolled and fought in an ecstasy
of living. (p. 229)

In this mood she compares Tormad and Roddie in her mind:

> Tormad was strong and instinctive, with the moods and
> graces of the instincts.
>   Roddie was strong and reasonable. (p. 229)

The opposition is not as simple as this suggests, though, for
since Tormad's death Catrine herself has changed: "the urgency
of her flesh had died down" (p. 229), and her spirit is quieter
though still passionate. She admits to herself that she has
been very close to accepting Roddie's advances, and knows
that the only thing holding Roddie back is the thought that
Tormad might still be alive. Catrine had not told Roddie she
believes Tormad is dead because she feels herself "weak" (p.
230) and is afraid, for all sorts of reasons, to begin a new
relationship.

She is distracted from such thoughts when Kirsty wakes
and we see the tenderness with which she cares for the older
woman, and the practicality of Kirsty's indomitable spirit. She
directs Catrine to a purse containing forty-one sovereigns,
and to a letter which will guarantee Catrine ownership of the
cottage after Kirsty's death. She also gives Catrine a very
direct piece of advice when she tells her not to try to keep Finn
from going to sea:

> "More ugly deaths on this land now than ever on sea. If you
> put [that] boy against his nature you'll warp him. Remember
> that." (p. 239)

It is ironic that this powerful piece of parenting advice comes
from the childless Kirsty, but it is typical of her clear-sight-
edness in general and of her knowledge of Catrine and Finn
in particular.

The chapter ends with Kirsty's death and, while Catrine is
trying to cope with the enormity of this, Finn's voice calls to
her from outside.

Chapter XII: Finn's Journey For A Doctor

Finn has returned from the journey he began at the end of
Chapter X, a journey of sixty miles on foot. The book is full of
journeys and here, despite the surface naturalism of the
description, Gunn uses the journey motif in a way that recalls
countless folk-tales:

> The night was short, and in the new world upon which the
> dawn came he found a stillness that sometimes enchanted
> him and sometimes made him a little afraid. (p. 243)

This is deliberate, and ties in with the way the book explores
how story carries meanings that go beyond the mere recount-
ing of events. Finn is very much on his own and feels out of
place socially, linguistically and geographically. Like the hero
in a quest tale Finn sets off to make a momentous journey in
which he will face terrible obstacles and learn much about
himself.

At the same time, Finn's journey shows his maturity, intelligence and modernity. He knows there is a new way to deal
with the plague, he knows roughly where he can find a doctor
who is doing this, and he is willing to put himself to the test
in order to save his mother. Even at a young age he is inde-
pendent enough to strike out on his own, and not simply rely
on Roddie's calm good sense because, although he values that
good sense, he knows it will take more than that to beat the
disease. Roddie has done his best with the cleansing rite but
Finn has more belief in modern medicine and science.

The journey is long and arduous and Finn is exhausted when
he finally reaches Wick. He is worn out with worry and
extremely self-conscious about his poor grasp of English,
worried that his Gaelic might not be understood. When he
reaches Wick he finds that the doctor is not at home and is
asked to come back in an hour. The whole experience of being
in Wick seems to him to be almost unreal:

> He tried not to gape, but his astonishment was very great,
> particularly at the number of shops and business premises,
> with their names in big lettering. (p. 250)

This brave new world is a far cry from the world of people cleared from the land and forced to forage for their very lives on the shore. The world has moved on since the day Tormad tentatively set out on his fateful journey in Chapter I. The harbour itself stopped his breath:

> Great stone walls, endless yards and cooperages, immense stacks of barrels, the smell of brine, long wooden jetties, the clanking of hammers, the loud rattling of wheels, warning yells and the cracking of whips, herring-guts, clouds of screaming gulls, women in stiff, rustling skirts, and everywhere men and boats. This was Wick, easy mistress of all the herring fisheries. Her population at the moment was increased by thousands of strangers, not only from Moray Firth ports like Buckie but from far-away townships of the Hebrides. (p. 250)

Gunn points out that Finn would normally avoid the sheer busyness of such a scene (p. 251), but his growing maturity shows through when instead of avoiding it he spends time making mental notes about boat construction. Despite his natural reticence Finn seems to be part of this new world.

The doctor and his colleague give Finn medicine to take back, and tell him that, if he saves his mother, he will not have to pay for it. However, the encounter with the doctor and his world is still slightly awkward as the medical men almost seem more interested in their research than in Finn, but the doctor's wife is very kind to him and explains more about how to deal with the cholera. He is particularly pleased when she explains that the house and belongings will not have to be destroyed in the old way, but just thoroughly cleaned. She gives him food, too, for the long journey back.

Chapter XIII: Ordeal By Plague

When Catrine hears Finn's voice in the darkness he has just returned from that journey and has brought the medicine for her and for Kirsty. He is terribly upset to hear Kirsty has died, but he forces himself to focus on convincing Catrine that she will survive. We can only imagine how he must feel leaving

her alone in the cottage with Kirsty's body while he goes back
to sleep at Roddie's. There is no sense of triumph in his having
made the journey, only exhaustion. He also feels inadequate
because he knows that while he is asleep Roddie will be talking
to Catrine across the burn at the cottage.

Next day a coffin is taken and left outside the cottage so
that Catrine can prepare Kirsty for burial. Here, and later
when Catrine has to drag the coffin back outside to be collected,
Gunn gives a very real sense of the physicality of the lives of
his characters. In his brittle state of mind, Finn is impressed
with Roddie as he watches him calmly organise events. Roddie
also suggests that when it is all over, if Catrine agrees, he will
take Finn to sea the following summer. He is also "strangely
moved" (p. 263) when he realises that Roddie has not been
fishing because he has stayed to help Catrine.

The tiredness and the tension, however, take their toll on
Finn, particularly when he realises that, like Kirsty, his mother
really could die. The realisation hits him hard:

> Like a stricken animal, he headed blindly for his private
> sanctuary, and, curled up in the shadows by the round ring
> of stones, he prayed that his mother would recover, not in
> words, but in the intensities that words destroy. (pp. 265–66)

As always, he goes back to the House of Peace for comfort and
consolation.

Next day Finn and Roddie visit the cottage together and, when
Catrine does not appear, Finn hot-headedly decides to go in to
see if she is all right. Roddie has to restrain him physically:

> "Listen, Finn. If you went in, what would your mother say?
> Damn it, boy, listen to me. Have sense. Do you want to go in
> and break her heart? [...] It's nothing for you or me to go in.
> That's easy. But what would your mother say? If she has the
> plague, God damn it, man, would it make her end easy to
> think she had given it to you, her son?" (p. 267)

In this whole episode Roddie has acted like a father to Finn,
and here he is teaching him a lesson in responsibility, a lesson

he has learned from a life at sea: there are things in life beyond man's control. Sometimes we have to learn to accept the inevitable and deal with the consequences.

Finn obeys Roddie's advice and Catrine survives. From this point on the novel focuses more and more on Finn's growth to maturity as an individual within his community.

Chapter XIV: Out To Sea

In this chapter we see Finn finally go to sea with his mother's blessing, although she had initially wanted him to go to university before realising that what Kirsty had said was true: it is in Finn's nature to go to sea. He is seventeen years old.

The chapter begins with Roddie and Finn and the crew of the *Seafoam* setting out from the beach with a crowd on the beach looking on because

> [...] this was the first time a Dunster boat was to venture beyond the Moray Firth. They were bound for Stornoway [...] (p. 271)

Perfectly naturalistic – such scenes would be common up and down the coast – the scene closely resembles the novel's opening scene and reminds us of Tormad's journey, of Catrine's fear, and of the excitement and wonder of such settings out. From the boat Finn sees a stranger approach his mother just as they are pulling out to sea. Later he discovers that it is Ronnie, one of Tormad's crew, who had been press-ganged with him on that original voyage. Ronnie's return is crucial to the development of the novel, as he confirms to Catrine that Tormad is dead.

The chapter is important in conveying to the reader, the feeling of being in an open boat at sea as they round Dunnett Head and make their way through the Pentland Firth before taking shelter in Loch Eriboll, a sea loch on Scotland's northern edge. Gunn is always skilled at evoking life outdoors, something that often goes un-noticed by critics who live in the urban centres. Here he describes very well the simple wonder of being on the sea and seeing the previously known world from a new perspective.

> It was pleasant to hear the water lapping and slapping against
> the bows. One would think the boat herself loved it, for if her
> head dipped it was only to rise again and be on, as a runner
> who trips will the more quickly speed. [...] The quiver of
> eagerness ran along her sides to the rudder, the sensitive
> rudder that sent the impulse to Roddie's hand [...] (p. 272)

The sense of the boat as a living creature is very strong here
and owes something to Gaelic literature which has a strong
tradition of poems celebrating boats, from "Birlinn Chlann
Raghnaill" ("The Birlinn of Clanranald") by Alasdair Mac
Mhaighistir Alasdair (Alexander MacDonald) in the eighteenth
century to "Siubhal a' Choire" ("The Voyaging of the Corrie")
and "Seeker Reaper" by Deòrsa Mac Iain Dheòrsa (George
Campbell Hay) in the twentieth.

The transition from the known to the unknown world is
handled very easily and naturally:

> Pleasant it was to see the land slipping by and the headland
> of home slowly closing on the stores, the yards, the beach,
> the river-mouth, like a gate closing in a dream until all their
> kindred were shut off, leaving them to adventure in the great
> expanses of the world. (p. 272)

This suggests one of the main methods of navigation without
compasses – memorising a coastline from the sea. It also
reminds us of the way Tormad and his crew watched the coast
in Chapter I.

Gunn is also very good at describing the interaction of the
various crew members, each of whom has recognisable character traits, and showing how Finn, the new boy, gradually
feels more and more relaxed and willing to join in the easy
banter of the older men. He is quietly pleased by this acceptance and feels that "his old shy self had opened" (p. 287).
Sleeping, or trying to sleep, in the open boat at Loch Eriboll,
lying on the nets and the folded sails in the rain and the swish
of the wind Finn finds "a soft warmth from fatigue suffused
his whole body; and on a last consciousness of the cradling
motion of the boat, he fell asleep" (p. 287).

"Cradling" suggests once again that Finn was born for this. He drifts in and out of sleep as he will do many times from now on when trying to rest between intense bursts of activity hauling nets or rowing hard. This moving in and out of consciousness also fits naturally into that level of the book concerned with dreams and the role of the unconscious in our lives.

Just as Gunn shows the easy-going relationships that exist between the various members of the crew, he also draws our attention several times to the way Roddie, the skipper, is seen as a man slightly apart:

> They saw him look at the sky, searching for the sun, for in between the showers its presence could be vaguely discerned in a dissipated silvery brightness. Then he settled to the tiller, his body upright, his eyes ahead [...] (p. 292)

Finn in particular is sharply aware of Roddie's presence:

> It was good to watch Roddie now, felt Finn. His eyes were like living drops of the ocean itself and you could see the exaltation of the fight concentrated in them. When they judged, and succeeded, the skin sometimes creased in fine ironic lines round the eyes, and once he looked at Finn suddenly, with a friendly smile, and said something with a quiet humour that Finn did not catch. (p. 296)

This is Roddie in his element, friendly and solicitous for his crew, especially for Finn on his first voyage, but responsibility for so many lives means there is also a strong core of inner strength and toughness. Watching the sea closely as the light begins to go, "Roddie's face went expressionless as stone." (p. 296) This is the side of Roddie Finn will have to face over the following pages.

Chapter XV: Storm and Precipice
Exciting and dramatic in itself, this is a crucial chapter in the developing relationship between Finn and Roddie, and marks a further advance in Finn's journey towards maturity.

In the dark of night they have to ride out a storm and are exhausted by the sheer physical effort:

> Whole hills of water seemed to come at them with great valleys between. For hours Roddie was cut off from his crew in a darkness as of winter. (p. 297)

Faced with such huge seas, which are described in landscape terms to emphasise the solidity and weight of the waves, the boat shudders, quivers, and chokes like a living thing in distress. Those of us who live on the land can have little idea of the power of such seas but here, as in *Morning Tide* and elsewhere, Gunn evokes for us the exhilaration, the fear, the exhaustion of it all. Finn's body is

> [...] battered into a heavy lassitude, so heavy indeed that when it relaxed completely, it felt light and incorporeal, and there came upon his spirit a fine clarity. (p. 298)

Watching the sea he begins to grasp how vulnerable the boat is to the movement of the waves. Yet he is not cowed by this. Instead he relishes the challenge. Again we see the difference between Finn and Tormad who never had the chance to take the measure of what to him was a new element.

As the storm dies down Roddie tells the crew he is not sure where they are and only when a ship appears do they find out they have gone much further than they had thought – beyond the Butt of Lewis, and into the North Atlantic. This was in the days before the lighthouse was built so in the darkness and the storm they had overshot Lewis. It is good to know where they are because they can alter course and head for Stornoway and safety but Finn is noticeably shaken by the sudden appearance of the ship which brings back all that he knows about Tormad and the press-gang (p. 302).

Heading for Stornoway, though, is not easy in this sea:

> Steering was a more delicate art than ever and Roddie's head seemed to get a curious swinging motion from the cross seas that bore down on them. For ever he had to be watchful, with

Chapter XVIII: Landing Herring

Finn returns to Stornoway and rejoins the others. Roddie is quiet and a rather uneasy peace prevails. He tells them he knows where there are herring and they set off to find them. On the way the old companionship comes back and the crew are pleased that Finn suggests to Roddie that he tells the skipper of the *Sulaire* about the fish too as he had earlier shared his catch with them. The boats return to port with a good catch and their success gives hope to others: "What one boat got to-day, another might get to-morrow" (p. 392).

Roddie is now being talked about with awe by the local fishermen, not just for the fight in the pub but also because of what they now acknowledge as "an incredible feat of seamanship in the Western Ocean" (p. 390) when he brought his crew safely back to Lewis after the storm.

Yet the three weeks' fishing that follows is hard and exhausting and takes its toll. Finn is still watching Roddie and is keenly aware that his "pleasantness was a mask, the sort of mask one did not try to penetrate" (p. 395). He has learned to distance himself from him:

> He became one of the crew, seeing Roddie as an objective body and presence with which it was no business of his to interfere. Roddie wanted no more trouble. Neither did he. (p. 396)

The effect of this is liberating as it means Finn is growing in maturity, and is more able to stand on his own two feet, with less reliance on authority figures.

The chapter ends with the *Seafoam* and her crew returning home, where no-one had heard about them since they left:

> Week after week – no news. That was good. They did not want news. They should be coming soon. Suddenly they would appear out of the sea – and be there. Like a miracle. (p. 405)

No news in those times meant good news. They were different days with no need for the modern obsession with constant communication. Finn has come home from the sea in a way his father was unable to do.

Chapter XIX: Sea Love

Catrine is delighted to see Finn and is very emotional when he gives her presents that show he had not forgotten about her. She is especially moved by the fact that he remembered to bring something for his cousin Barbara, who had been helping her on the croft in his absence. Gunn gives a moving picture of the return home, with lots of restrained emotion and no over-demonstrativeness. Finn is pleased to be home, but also a little awkward. He goes out to the barn with its "old, stuffy smell [and] overwhelming familiarity" (p. 408). His journey has unsettled him:

> Slowly he looked round at the odds and ends and saw them with an extreme distinctness. He was here and he was not here, as if there was one world behind the other. But all the time he knew he must go in. (p. 408)

When he does go in, he is "relieved and happy" (p. 409) and entertains Catrine and Barbara with his presents and his stories.

Later, when they are on their own, Catrine tells him that the man who had approached her on the beach the day he set sail was Ronnie, who had been press-ganged with Tormad (p. 410). Ronnie had told Catrine how Tormad had been injured that day and had died five days later. He was buried at sea. She tells Finn that she had always known he was dead because he came to her the night he died. Finn is deeply upset, not just about Tormad's death but because of the unfair nature of his death. When he regains his composure and they walk back to the house:

> [...] a deep feeling came over him of being himself and his own father, responsible for this woman walking by his side, who was his mother [...] (p. 411)

In the time after his return life is good. He works hard on the croft and gets ready for the summer fishing. But he is

shocked when he hears that a young boy has been badly injured
on the cliffs, playing a game based on his exploits on the Seven
Hunters (p. 412). Finn had not bragged of this, but his story
had become part of local lore through the talk of others. The
boys of the village look up to him as a kind of hero.

He takes to the summer fishing with relish:

> It was the height of summer, and the night never grew quite
> dark. Finn loved to feel the gentle movement of the boat
> under him again. (p. 413)

On the sea, busy with work, he can avoid Una and all the
awkward complications of young love. Una seems to be involved
with a boy called Jim, and seems to have no interest in Finn.
He regards it as a weakness to be troubled by thoughts of her.

One night, when he is in company with Jim and Una and
Betz and Donnie, he finds himself walking Betz back home. He
is unhappy at this and does not want to talk to her but after
practically ignoring her for a while he catches a sense of her as
"sensitive and timid and unsure of herself" (p. 425). To his credit
he feels mean and ashamed of himself and begins to pay attention to her as a real person. This is another powerful moment
in his growth to maturity, as he acknowledges his selfishness
and begins to behave more generously to someone who lacks
his own apparently secure sense of worth and self-esteem.

However, he feels embarrassed in front of the others and
when he leaves them he heads for Hendry's pub consumed
with anger. After some drinks he asks Special for a bottle of
whisky and is refused. He heads off for a house where he
thinks he will be able to get drink but finding Jim there
he punches him. (p. 428) The moment echoes the way Roddie
had struck Finn in Stornoway, and Gunn points out that the
other boys "had seen the flash and movement of the sea in
him" (p. 429). After this he goes home drunk, but not before
going to the House of Peace in a spirit of defiance, challenging
it to bring forth its ghosts. He almost passes out when he sees
a "grey-white movement" among the stones and an "icy coldness
went to [his] heart" (p. 430). This is no ghost, however, just
another crofter's wandering goat.

Next day he and Jim make up, as Finn feels rather ashamed of himself. He tells Jim:

"I don't care for girls. They're a waste of time." (p. 432)

a statement that echoes Roddie's earlier

"I have married the sea." (p. 133)

He is glad to get back to the all-male world of the *Seafoam*, but finds that news of his escapade has again been spread abroad. It seems that Finn, like Roddie, is a person people notice.

Part of his attraction is his single-minded devotion to the sea, which comes to dominate his every thought:

[The sea] was a stupendous thing in itself. The mere handling of a boat against it was a thrill that nothing on land, in man or in woman, could equal. (p. 435)

He begins to put thoughts of Una out of his mind because he cannot deal with them, cannot fathom her. On the sea, in a boat, life makes sense to him. The world of the emotions is much too complex and unknowable for him. Instead of thinking about Una he develops an "obsession" (p. 434) to own his own boat and skipper his own crew.

Chapter XX: Finn Goes to Helmsdale

Finn accompanies Barbara back to Helmsdale, which has seen great changes since Catrine left. In the ceilidh-house Finn is asked to tell the story of his Hebridean voyage. He does this well, because he is able to pace his story and to use dramatic pauses and dramatic language where it is appropriate. He tells his tale with style, in a way that links him to the storytellers of the past who had to engage their audiences through the power of their language. We are in the days before television, cinema, and the computer. We are just about at the very beginning of photography, so pictures had to be created by words. Finn proves that, even as a young man, he is a master of this.

Part of the mastery lies in the community's acceptance of him as one of their own. He is, in a way, speaking for them, not putting on a performance suggesting he is somehow better than them. They appreciate this and when his voice falters as he describes the appearance of the strange ship, they understand his emotion because many of them had known his father and knew what had happened to him. Interestingly, Finn discovers his ability in storytelling as he tells his story. In telling the story, his own creative engagement with his experience re-creates it in the minds of his listeners, many of whom had also spent much time at sea and understood very well the incidents and scenes that he describes. He is complimented on his storytelling abilities because the Gaelic culture of that time really valued the power of the storyteller.

The very next day Finn is given more insight into the power of story when Ronnie comes to see him and tells him about his father's death. Ronnie is quiet and serious. He begins by telling Finn he is sorry not to have heard his story the night before; then, as they walk up the strath of Kildonan, he tells Finn all about the place. He describes scenes from his youth with Catrine and Tormad, and tells Finn about the clearing of the people from the land. Finn is shy and modest with Ronnie because he knows that Ronnie has travelled the world and seen many places and many strange things. It makes his own story about the Hebrides seem less impressive, although that is not Ronnie's intention.

There is, however, an odd sadness in Ronnie's story as he says he did not find much in the wider world except violence, greed and brutality. Being taken forcibly from his own place meant that he had held it in his mind as a sustaining vision of a kind of paradise with which nothing could compare. The longer he held that vision, though, the more it would become unreal, for the place he remembered was changing all the time he was away from it. Ronnie also admits that he too gave in to brutality and weak behaviour, something he is not proud of. He is really a shell of the young man he once was. He tells Finn he would have courted Catrine when they were young because she was beautiful and full of life:

"But I had no chance with her, when your father was about!"
(p. 453)

When he goes on to describe the press-ganging and Tormad's
death Finn pictures it all just as those in the ceilidh-house
had visualised his own story. Ronnie lacks Finn's ability with
language, but his story hits home because of its stark simplic-
ity, and the authority that comes from having lived through
what he is describing.

He finishes by complimenting Finn, and counselling him
against going away from this place in search of position or
power or money. He has recognised Finn's thirst for adventure,
and when he mentions his story of the night before, Finn says
quietly and modestly

"That was nothing." (p. 454)

compared to what Ronnie had been through. Ronnie says simply,

"It took you to the edge of death – and further than that no
adventure can travel in this life." (p. 455)

The conversation ends with Ronnie suggesting that Finn take
a sprig of rowan berries for Catrine, to remind her of the strath
where she had grown up, to

"[...] show her you remembered her." (p. 455).

They would probably also remind her of Ronnie.

Finn leaves Helmsdale to return home in good spirits. People
had been kind to him, and he could see that

[...] people [were] happy again, with the coming of prosperity
from the sea. The sea did not belong to any landlord and the
use of the press-gang was dying out. (pp. 455–56)

The world has changed radically even in the short time since
his birth. It is now a world for young men, and Finn is exhorted
to drive it forward. It is a challenge he cannot ignore.

Chapter XXI: Catrine and Roddie

After Finn and Barbara leave for Helmsdale Catrine finds herself on her own and because of this she reflects quietly on her life. In this chapter she confronts and deals with many of her inner demons.

> Catrine was now thirty-eight, a fully-developed woman, her shoulders rounded and firm, her chest deep, her face more full than it had been in the old days but with the eyes still large and the mouth red. The texture of her fair skin retained much of the smoothness of youth, of girlhood. (p. 458)

Despite all that has happened to her she is still a very attractive woman. In this she is contrasted sharply with Ronnie whose life at sea has ground him down and taken much of the life out of him. He is attracted to her because of her looks and personality, but also because she represents the youth which had been so brutally taken from him by the press-gang. For Ronnie, most of the excitement of life is over. He is keenly aware that most of his life is past and he has lost his vitality. Catrine is still very much alive. She had rejected Ronnie's advances because, although he is a pleasant, thoughtful and considerate man, she knew she "would never get away from the past with Ronnie" (p. 461). Her strength of character, her sense of survival and self-preservation is very strong. That is why, without ever betraying her past, she has moved on in her life in a way that Ronnie has found impossible. Bringing up her son has been crucial to that process of moving on. Coping with his changing moods means that the process is not yet over, and she is still very much involved in Finn's life.

Yet, left on her own in the cottage, she thinks about Roddie too and how he "had made up his mind to leave her alone" (p. 465). She sees this as "the end of another chapter in her life" (p. 465) and in a moment of despair feels her own essential alone-ness, what Gunn calls her "ultimate loneliness. [...] It was her first real intimation of Death" (p. 466). In this mood she prepares to spend the night alone in the empty house. It

is a night of anxiety, terror and hysteria as she imagines the
ghosts of Kirsty and her father coming back to haunt her. By
the flickering and flitting light of her candle,

> [...] she thought she saw, over against the farthest wall, the
> figure of Kirsty's father, standing quite straight, with a look
> of remote yet infinite understanding in his grey face. (p. 469)

The similarity with the figure Finn imagined at the House of
Peace and in the cell at the Seven Hunters is striking. Both
Catrine and Finn seem to have access to another way of seeing
the world in which they live.

The terror and anxiety of the night give way to a lighter
mood in the morning and Catrine begins to get the house ready
for Finn's return (p. 471). Her love of her son and her pride
in him are tempered by her awareness that an overly emotional
display of that love would be inappropriate. This contrasts
with her outburst in Chapter I when she tried to prevent
Tormad from going to sea.

Roddie looks in on her and they chat pleasantly before he
goes, leaving her "full of intense dismay" (p. 474) as she realises
that despite her earlier insight she is still attracted to him,
but cannot work out if he is still attracted to her. It flashes
upon her mind that

> [...] certain little acts and attitudes of Finn towards Roddie,
> small intangible affairs mostly which she had put down to
> manhood's normal growth in her son, now became clear. Finn
> was jealous of Roddie; and Roddie was intolerant of Finn.
> Because of her! (p. 475)

She thinks this through and thinks it will be easy to put things
right between Finn and Roddie. She decides that as Finn is
trying to buy his own boat she will give him half of the money
Kirsty had given her:

> If there was this folly between Roddie and himself, the sooner
> he had a boat of his own the better. (p. 476)

The thought brings contentment to her troubled mind and suffuses her body with warmth:

> She felt the rich flow of life in her flesh. Lately her body had had this deep warm feeling of well-being very strongly. Her skin had the fairness that holds light. Her hair was fair. In the peat fire, her brown eyes looked black and gleamed with lights. [...] She looked like a woman whose mind is made up, who is content, because she is waiting for her lover. There was that faint, expectant, almost wanton air about her. (p. 477)

The image of Catrine on the stool by the fire occurs again and again in the book. The mood it evokes this time is very different from all the others. It is also slightly ambiguous. Who is she waiting for: Finn or Roddie? Neither comes that night, but Roddie comes when she is milking Bel the next day and she gives herself to him in "the stall with the straw, where Finn had been born" (p. 478).

Chapter XXII: Finn Denies His Mother
Finn had been held up on his journey because he took a detour to the House of Peace. He is a little ashamed of his previous visit under the influence of drink so he needs to re-establish his normal relationship with the place. He is tired but happy to be home and after resting for a little while makes his way back to the cottage. That is where he encounters Catrine and Roddie coming out of the byre together.

The meeting is awkward and his mood of contentment at coming home and Catrine's eagerness to welcome him are immediately swept away as he tries to understand the situation. Roddie leaves and Finn and Catrine are left alone making awkward conversation with many awkward pauses. The small kitchen becomes silent but filled with an awful tension. Finn takes the sprig of rowan berries from Kildonan out of his pocket:

> He regarded them on his palm with a slow sarcasm, then pitched them towards the fire, but with a physical indiffer-

ence that let them fall short, an indifference that yet had in
it an odd perversity, as though he would not quite destroy
them, but must let them be seen. (p. 482)

He is aware of "an extraordinary stillness" (p. 482) in the
room and feels he cannot look at his mother. The dull, obsti-
nate refusal, the silent battle of wills as each of them will not
or cannot speak to each other has been seen several times
before. It is a situation and a feeling that readers recognise
from their own lives. What breaks the mood is that Catrine
collapses:

> She hit the floor with a solid thump, and lay with the crown
> of her head a couple of inches from the sharp edge of the
> hearthstone. (p. 482)

Finn is completely shocked and is extremely agitated as he
tries to bring her round. His love for her takes over from his
other confused feelings about her and Roddie and he carefully
lets her come to and regain her composure. He picks up the
berries which had so affected her because of all the past
memories they had brought to her mind. He goes outside to
calm down, but is plagued by thoughts of Roddie and his
mother which he does not want to face so he puts them aside
and "[a]fter that his expression grew cunning and full of a
bitter mockery" (p. 485). When he returns to the house everything carries on as normal, but beneath the apparent calmness
there is a great deal of tension.

Next day Catrine talks to Roddie and admits that she is
afraid Finn will pick a fight with him:

> "If there was any trouble between you – it would kill me".
> (p. 487)

She asks him to stay away for a little while. Roddie, on the
other hand, thinks they should simply tell Finn about their
developing relationship. Catrine knows that Finn will find it
hard to accept and is afraid and possibly embarrassed about
telling him:

A feeling of intense shame came upon her [...] Visions would come back. She crushed them into the grass. Everything was wrong. Life was ugly and miserable. She had been so happy with Finn alone. (p. 488)

Critics sometimes claim that Gunn does not deal with the "darkness" that afflicts many people's lives. Here he is looking at it head on. Catrine is living two hundred years ago when social *mores* were very different. An unmarried woman or a widow involved in a sexual relationship would be looked down on by the whole community. Part of her knows she has done nothing wrong, but when she re-imagines making love to Roddie she can hardly acknowledge that that was her, and that that was what she wanted. Her whole upbringing is telling her it is wrong. Because of this her life seems completely blighted. Yet in acknowledging that it was easier when it was just Finn and herself alone, she is admitting that she is afraid to live her own life separate from her son. If Finn has been learning how to live as himself, as a mature individual, by going to sea, then Catrine will have to learn to do the same: live her own life as a fully mature individual.

That is why Gunn shows her beginning to change even as she feels at her lowest ebb:

[...] behind this emotion her mind was gathering its cunning, which knew neither shame nor bitterness, only the real knowledge of life as it was [...] (p. 488)

For Catrine, for Gunn, cunning is a very real and necessary attitude to bring to bear on the world if we are to survive. Many people would see cunning as a negative quality or attribute. This is not the way Gunn sees it, which gives an added complexity to his characterisation of Catrine and of Finn. At this point in the book, with Catrine embarking on a sexual relationship with Roddie, with neither Finn nor Catrine really wanting to acknowledge this and the way it alters their relationship, we are very far away from the very real but uncomplicated relationship between Catrine and Finn early in the book.

The next section of the chapter (pp. 488–92) shows Finn avoiding his home and his mother as much as he can and spending more and more time at the beach with men and boats. A conversation there gives some of the astonishing figures that mark the economic success of the herring fishing. Not only do the fishermen make money, but many other people are employed in the industry. Again the sharp contrast is with the extreme poverty of Finn's own people at the beginning of the book when, cleared from their land, they had to forage for food in an alien landscape. Everything seems bright and only one man stops to ask,

"Ay, but will it last?" (p. 491)

We know now that it did not last, or that it lasted for a while then went into a decline, as all things must. Gunn's first novel, *The Grey Coast* (1926), was set against the background of this decline. The chapter ends when, on his way back to the croft:

[...] he heard his mother's voice cry out [...] It was a strange, sharp, heart-wrung cry. Roddie's head and back appeared. He had Catrine in his arms, bearing her lightly, and he was laughing. (p. 493)

Despite Roddie trying to speak to him, Finn turns and walks off to lie down in a small wood nearby until darkness falls. He seems numbed and because he does not want to face the thought of Roddie and Catrine together, does not even want to think about it enough to reject it. He begins to feel very very alone and isolated, alienated from everything around him. In this mood he wanders over the moor in the darkness like a ghost. He pauses at two ceilidh-houses but does not go in. It is as if he is deliberately cutting himself off from the social life of his community. He wanders on in his self-imposed isolation, then stops at Una's house where, unobserved, he looks through her window and sees

[...] a young woman with her back to him, sitting on a small stool just beyond the fire, making a net. Her right hand was

> extremely dexterous and the white bone needle flew out and
> in. [...] There were others, but Finn could not take his eyes
> off this stranger, this dark young woman with her hair up.
> All at once, she turned her head over her shoulder and looked
> at the window. [...] He saw her eyes open, her expression
> grow rigid in terror, and at once he tip-toed away. (p. 494)

This is almost sinister, as in that culture, as Gunn points out, when a girl hears her name called from outside at night it presages her death. Finn knows he had not called her name, but he realises that if she had seen him she would think it was "his wraith" (p. 494).

He next rows out to a schooner that is lying at anchor with the intention of signing up for a voyage – exactly what Ronnie had advised him against doing – but he is too late. The ship has a full complement. The incident shows Finn's desperation, and his immaturity (p. 495). It also deepens his depression and he admits to being revolted by the obscenity of the image of his mother's "heavy elderly body [...] in Roddie's arms" (p. 495). His inability to deal with the fact of his mother as a sexual being is another sign of his immaturity, as is his continual putting out of his mind any thoughts of Una. He is obviously attracted to her but seems afraid at some very deep level to admit it. Possibly, like Catrine earlier, he feels that life is easier if lived on one's own.

When he eventually returns home, Catrine is waiting up for him, sitting on the stool in front of the fire. They exchange a few desperate words as neither really knows how to deal with the situation. When Catrine tells him that she and Roddie are to be married, Finn says it has nothing to do with him and walks away into his room, shutting the door behind him and leaving the house filled with "a silence intense and desolate" (p. 497).

Chapter XXIII: The Wreck
Catrine and Roddie are married and Finn begins to distance himself even more from them, as if by ignoring them he will not have to face up to the fact of his mother's sexuality. For Finn it is a great relief when the wedding is over and he no

longer has to pretend to be happy in their company. He "never wanted to have anything more to do with them, had for them a cold distaste" (p. 500). He is aware that he has changed a lot in body and in mind although he is barely twenty (p. 500). His body has hardened and so has his heart. When his mother moves to live in Roddie's house and Finn is offered Catrine's croft he wants nothing to do with it, nor with the money she offers him, because of his pride. Soon, though, the calculating, grown-up part of him realises that it would just be stupid and childish to refuse. The realisation that he could have his own croft, his own house, and his own boat gives him a sense of power (p. 502), a definite sense of his own manhood.

This side of Finn can be seen too in the way he is keen to develop the cod and ling fishing. This had been happening in Dunster already but "in Finn's view the business had been too easy-going, not taken seriously enough" (pp. 502–03). With his new sense of purpose he works out how to fish for cod and ling in a more profitable way, which enables him to break with Roddie, who does not want to engage in it. Several echoes can be caught here – Tormad's tentative first voyage which had no real sense of direction or purpose, and Roddie's shy early negotiations with Hendry described in Chapter IV where the contrast between the practical fisherman and the entrepreneurial Hendry is very sharp. Finn, it seems, has no qualms about making money. In this he is, like Hendry, much more "modern" than Tormad and Roddie who are representatives of an older world. There is a contrast too between Finn's youth and drive to succeed, and Roddie's steady sense of fulfilment in his marriage, a feeling that he no longer has to prove himself. With his marriage his priorities have shifted. With the arrogant certainty of youth Finn sees this as weakness on Roddie's part. As Roddie is drawn less and less to the sea, Finn is more and more drawn to it and goes to it in a spirit of testing himself against it. He has taken on Roddie's toughness but lacks his balanced calmness:

> The weather was often wet and stormy, and occasionally it was intensely, bitterly cold. For spells, feeling would desert his hands and even the flesh on his back, and the cold would

crawl along his bones. [...] Not only his hands but his mind seemed washed by the cold sea water. (p. 505)

This is Finn the penitent, trying to cleanse himself of impurities through the harshness of work. Yet even here there is evasion and self-deception, for he is using the sea as a way of escaping from thinking about Catrine and Roddie. And Una. For all his maturity as a brave and daring seaman, it seems Finn is afraid of his sexuality, and of the vulnerability that comes with giving oneself to another. At this point in his life he is a confused and unattractive character.

Yet it is out of this confusion and pretence that the real Finn emerges, in an incident that involves his acting selflessly on behalf of the community and which brings Roddie and himself closer. When a boat founders at the foot of the cliffs during a storm the people's mood of helplessness is broken when Finn decides to go down the cliff-face on a rope and attempt a rescue. In an image that contrasts vividly with their previous encounter with a cliff-face, Roddie controls the rope from the top, the two men thus bringing together their outstanding and contrasting qualities – the audacity of youth and the calmness of experience. Their own recognition of this is a moving acknowledgement of their separate strengths and weaknesses, and an acknowledgement of their need for each other:

> "Are you ready?" asked Finn, and he met Roddie's eyes.
> "Will you try it, boy?" asked Roddie, and his voice was gentle.
> It was a moment of communion so profound that Finn felt a light-heartedness and exaltation come upon him. This was where Roddie and himself met, in the region of comradeship that lies beyond all the trials of the world. (p. 513)

The description of the storm is vivid and intense and intensely physical as Gunn describes the overwhelming power of the wind and the waves which constantly reminds us of the fragility of human bodies when facing the violence of a universe that pays no heed to human comfort. Some of Gunn's descriptions are sharply reminiscent of Scottish paintings of sea and

shore from MacTaggart to Eardley in their panoramic vision
of the scene:

> Already folk were appearing from the crofts, men and women
> and boys. Small boats were being drawn up the beach by
> seamen wet to the waists. Women with heads tightly shawled
> leaned against the storm, their wide skirts flapping. The
> seadrift whistled past in a stinging rain. Blobs of spume big
> as gulls' eggs caught the ground, shivered and burst. (p. 509)

Roddie himself appears to Finn almost to be part of the
landscape, "[s]tanding on an outer skerry [...] with a coil of
rope in his hand" (p. 509) as the helpless watchers on shore
can see the efforts of the four men in the boat "pulling out to
sea with the utmost strength of their bodies, pulling into the
eye of the wind and being driven before it" (pp. 509–10). The
small boat is helpless in the grip of the wind and the waves
and Roddie and the others cannot get close enough to help
them. It is a heartbreaking scene that has been seen round
the coasts of these islands for centuries. Finn knew the crew
well:

> They moved, living, in Finn's mind, and it was incredible to
> him that they should now die, smashed against the cliffs and
> drawn down into the green water. (p. 512)

Yet as Gunn knew from growing up as the son of a fisherman
on that northern coast, this was the harsh reality of life for
fishermen in small boats in dangerous and unpredictable
waters.

When Finn goes down the cliff with Roddie holding the rope
at the top and directing the others he relies on touch to guide
him in the noise and batter of the wind and the flying spindrift
while Roddie relies on the feel of the rope in his hands to tell
him how Finn is doing. Two men are saved but two are lost.
One of the men saved is Una's brother, Duncan. Desperate
attempts to revive him come to no avail and even Roddie
almost gives up hope after thirty minutes of working on the
body, but the boy's mother will not give up:

> Then they saw Duncan's mother do a thing that silently and
> strangely moved them all. Anticipating Roddie's order to
> chafe the feet, she stripped the boots off and the two pairs
> of thick socks, and then with a curious whimper, she unfas-
> tened her bodice and placed the cold lifeless feet between
> her deep breasts, and covered them over with the bodice,
> and pressed them inward, while the tears flowed down her
> face and she murmured, "My boy! my own boy!" (pp. 518–19)

When everyone else has given up only the boy's mother has
any hope left, and she is rewarded when she feels life coming
back to him. It is an uplifting and heartening moment in an
episode that leaves the small community shocked and stunned
by the loss of two of its young men.

Chapter XXIV: As The Rose Grows Merry in Time
After the rescue Finn knows he is a changed man. The close
encounter with death has given him a quieter sense of himself,
as he knows nothing else can be as unknowable or as frighten-
ing (p. 525), so when he sets off for Stornoway with his new
crew in the *White Heather* there is a new warmth in him.
Enjoying the brightness of the day he experiences the same
wonder when looking back at the land from the sea that his
father had experienced on his fateful voyage all those years
ago:

> [...] the odd sensation of seeing all that belonged to [the
> land] both diminished and made clear in its proportions.
> (pp. 525–26)

The new sense of proportion extends also to Roddie and Catrine,
and to his "desperate, terrifying feelings" about them, which
he sees now as "an odd sort of madness" (p. 526) which can
still trouble him but which is fading in its intensity so that he
feels free to live his own life.

Stornoway, however, has about it an air of defeat; a lack of
enthusiasm for the herring fishing as opposed to "the tolerable
certainty of the cod and ling season, backed up, as June came
in, by the kelp-burning" (p. 531). Money had been lost to

unscrupulous dealers and curers and the people lacked the will to try again. The locals are astonished when the *White Heather* sets out to hunt for herring on a dirty-looking night. The bad weather, however, forces them to make a landing on North Uist. It is to be a pivotal place in Finn's story.

North Uist is a special place because it seems like "a forgotten place that had lived on" (p. 536). For all his modernity and drive, Finn is attracted by some of the traditional ways of this place. The people are friendly and hospitable in the old style and in return for their hospitality the crew of the *White Heather* help them gathering the seaweed from the shore for use as a valuable fertiliser. Finn enjoyed this work and the interaction with the community young and old. The old man in whose house Finn sleeps tells him much of the lore and traditions of the place. He is one of the tradition-bearers of the district, and has a profound effect on Finn, who has done his own share of storytelling:

> [Finn] could have listened to him for hours on end, because as he listened something in himself that had hitherto been dry, like dry soil, was moistened as by summer rain, and became charged with an understirring of life [...] (p. 538)

The arrival of Finn and his crew is itself a story that "had a quickening on the lives of these folk" (p. 539) as they gathered together in the evening, keen for news of the world beyond. In the days before the internet, before television and cinema and radio, this was often how people got their news. It is in such a setting that Finn tells the story of his first journey to the West. And it is definitely now a story, a deliberately honed narrative, that brings out the drama of that trip for others to share in or wonder at (p. 540). Later, the old storyteller, whose name is also Finn, compliments him graciously on his story:

> "You told the story well. You brought us into the far deeps of the sea and we were lost with you in the Beyond where no land is, only wind and wave and the howling of the darkness. You kept us in suspense on the cliffs, and you had some art in the way you referred to our familiars of the other

world before you told of the figure of the man you felt by the
little stone house. There you saw no-one and you were anxious
to make this clear, smiling at your fancy. It was well enough
done. It was all well done. It was done, too, with the humour
that is the play of drift on the wave. And you were modest."
(p. 540)

This could almost be a description of *The Silver Darlings* itself,
and gives something of the novelist's imperative to put the
reader or listener inside the reality of his created world so
that by experiencing it, even vicariously, his life is enriched
and opened out. Transformed. It is a large claim, but one that
old Finn hints at when he tells the young man that there was
something else in his story, something he will not know or
understand until he is as old as himself and sees it through
his eyes. Alike in name, yet so different in age and experience,
the two show the same kind of continuity of life that Gunn
has tracked through Tormad, Finn and Roddie. Each is his
own man, but each is part of a larger community of individuals. The section ends with old Finn's enigmatic statement that

"Many a one may come [...] in the guise of the stranger"
(p. 540)

implying that there is something in young Finn of the Celtic
hero Finn MacCoul and of Christ.[1]
Song, as well as story, also has a profound effect on Finn in
North Uist. When he hears a girl singing in a ceilidh house
he is immediately transported by her song:

It was a lullaby his mother had sung to him on the green
brae with its bushes and birds above the little stream in the
time of the herding. (p. 543)

Unconscious memories of his mother and himself in that far-off
time break upon him and he is filled with a sense of her uncon-
ditional love for him. The reader, too, remembers that time
from earlier in the novel and appreciates the way Catrine is
linked to the land rather than the sea which is Finn's element.

In her marriage to Roddie perhaps land and sea are brought
into a dynamic balance. When it is Finn's turn to sing he sings
a song in which a young girl pledges her love for a boy once
he has carried out a series of impossible tasks. It is a reminder
of the folk-tale element of the book and suggests both the
difficulty of winning the heart of Una, and Finn's unconscious
recognition that that is what he has to do.

In coming to accept the strength of his own feelings he also
begins to accept Catrine as she is:

> He was fond of her, would ever have for her a natural affec-
> tion, but he saw her now as a woman under the spell of her
> own destiny. (p. 549)

His feelings for Una are very different, and so strong that he
can no longer evade them without going against his own nature.
Something in the girl's song had brought this home to him.

Story, in the form of rumour and speculation, also plays its
role when the *White Heather* is wrongly thought to have gone
down in a storm off the Shiant islands, and their time in the
West ends when the crew sail her into Stornoway harbour
laden with herring. It is a bright end to Finn's new venture.

Chapter XXV: The Birch Wood
They return home to a great welcome, as the rumour that they
had perished off the Shiants had somehow reached home
before them:

> It was a tremendous moment for those who had gone through
> days of fear and despair [...] It was not every day the beloved
> dead come home alive. (pp. 556–57)

It is a moment that has happened over and over in fishing
communities round Scotland's coast, but in the case of Finn,
son of Tormad, it has added resonance and is again part of
that level of the book which touches on folk and fairy tale.

Things at home have changed, too. Roddie and Catrine have
had a baby. When Finn visits them he is embarrassed at the
way Roddie fusses over it in a way that in those days would

have been seen as "unmanly", but which most modern readers will find touching as it shows the older man's genuine love of his new baby and suggests a hitherto unnoticed quality of tenderness in him.

Finn gives presents to everyone and the occasion is happy if slightly restrained. Only when he produces the present he had brought for the new baby does Catrine break down and show real emotion, as she is so pleased. Roddie thanks him, with his "old remote smile" and says the gesture was worth more to him and Catrine than a thousand pounds. (pp. 562–63) After this Finn goes on his way feeling rather lonely, but glad that he had brought the present for the new baby. (p. 563) He is still wrestling with his feelings about Roddie and Catrine but he is making a huge effort to enter into their lives again.

A week later Finn goes to the House of Peace. He is "tired and wretched" (p. 563) and has gone there for solace; he cannot really understand why he feels like this, since in less than two days he is to take delivery of his new boat, the *Gannet*. Only when he imagines being at sea in her does his mind clear:

> [...] he saw the clean green seas running [...] He would be all right when he looked at the lifting stem of his own boat. Then would come upon him a freedom that would have in it the gaiety of revenge over all the cluttering doubts and anxieties of the earth. (p. 563)

On his own Finn can live a life that is free of social and sexual complications and entanglements and confusions. To open himself up to tenderness and intimacy is to make himself vulnerable in a way that he has always found difficult. Even here, at the place which has sustained him throughout his life, he can find no peace of mind. That will come only when he has penetrated all his self-deceptions and evasions to the core. This is the real rite of purgation and in the centre of his being Finn must fully acknowledge Una and all she represents, as she is the only one able to penetrate the circle of his defences. In the end he has to acknowledge this, and in a full acceptance of the wholeness of his own individuality, encompassing every facet of his personality, he is able to acknowledge his need for Una.

When he goes to her, Gunn echoes the moment in Chapter XXI when he had watched her from the wood behind her cottage and seen her look up apprehensively when she suspected she was being watched and feared hearing her name being called from beyond – a sure sign of approaching death. Late at night he watches Una finishing off the day's work and calls her name as he steps out from the cover of the wood. Una goes to him but in a strange mood Finn does not understand until she eventually reveals her terror at hearing her name being called:

> "To-night, *when I heard my name called* – and looked up – and saw you standing still against the wood, with only your hand beckoning me—" (p. 569)

She has faced death to be with Finn, and he is moved to the core by her courage, and the strength of her love for him.

Chapter XXVI: Finn in the Heart of the Circle
The last chapter echoes the first, with significant variations, as if to emphasise the continuity of life while acknowledging its changes. Finn collects his new boat, the *Gannet*, and takes her out on the sea. Unlike his father in the first chapter, Finn is an assured and accomplished seaman, and relishes the chance to see what the boat can do. Gunn's language here is again reminiscent of Gaelic praise-poems to boats:

> They saw his eyes gleam through the faint smile on his face that was lifted to the horizon. And he put her into it; he baptized her; he brought the strong spray over her bows; he lay her over until the sea seethed along her lee rail [...] She was very clean and sweet in her gleaming tar and new paint and grained wood of mast and oar, as she turned and flew before the wind. (p. 571)

He is pleased with her and sails her for home, again bringing to our minds the contrast between his voyage and Tormad's fateful voyage *away* from home in Chapter I. Finn, too, is sailing towards his love Una, while Tormad sailed away from Catrine. On their journey home along the coast his crew look out for the familiar fishermens' landmarks. Finn is looking out for the Birch Wood near where Una lives. The shore is crowded with people who have been watching out for their return. The whole chapter is full of such echoes and variations on previous scenes in the story of the community.

Drawing closer to the end of his novel, Gunn celebrates "the gleam of human life" (p. 573) by evoking once more the sheer bustle and excitement of a busy harbour: the babble of voices from many different communities drawn together in the new enterprise, from Lewis, from Wick, from Banffshire, all with their different rhythms and sounds.

> Bodies threading the maze of the busy hours of landing and gutting, the gleam of human life. (p. 573)

Many of the book's characters make cameo appearances as they are all part of the life of the community for *The Silver Darlings* is as much a novel about community as it is about its individual characters learning how to live their separate individual lives.

In this novel which celebrates the importance in our lives of storytelling Gunn's narrative also ebbs and flows like the sea. Finn's first fishing season with his new boat is a good one, but overall it was not a "markedly successful season" (p. 573) for everyone, which brings a touch of melancholy to this last chapter. This mood is continued in the lovely description of Finn alone with his thoughts in the boat with his crew resting all around him:

> [...] Finn was invaded by a sleepless calm that left him inclined to sit and stare. Perhaps it was an aftermath of the sunset that had turned the clouds into vast banks of fiery red. The sky had indeed come alive in a wild and menacing beauty, and all the sea had run red in molten currents, and the red had come off the sea and shone in the faces of the silent crew and glittered in their eyes. (p. 574)

The sun sets and the sky turns leaden and oppressive while gulls cry and float past "ghost-white against the black rock"

(p. 574) of the coastline. In the quietness of the darkening
Finn can see all the other boats, over a hundred of them, far
off to the east. He worries that he has come too far in his desire
to fish where he can see Una's cottage, which he thinks of as
a lucky talisman. In the strange quietness he thinks of the
"extreme entrancement" (p. 575) of her eyes before he is brought
back to his normal self by a strange sight:

> [...] a large patch of glassy light on the dark sea. [...] this
> shape took the likeness of a woman's head and shoulders
> [...] (p. 575)

The shape moves as if bowing to his nets, and he realises it is
the movement of a shoal of herring whose phosphorescence
he has been watching:

> [...] the flame ran into sheets, swift evanescent fires, with
> the pale green light that is sometimes seen in the moon; but
> more intense, and always vanishing, elusive [...] (p. 576)

The first net comes up empty, but soon the other nets are full
of

> [...] swirls of light [...] a little silver dance [...] banks of show
> that swayed in living mass, throwing off spindrift of elfin-
> green light. [...] And they came [...] fluttering up out of the
> sea, the silver darlings, dancing in over the gunnel with small
> thin cries. (pp. 576–77)

Finn's decision to shoot his nets away from the main part
of the fleet has paid off and the *Gannet* takes a full load of
fish. Waiting on the shore, Una is profoundly moved by this:

> The dark eyes glimmered deeply, and an irrational happiness
> quivered, all in an instant, on the verge of tears. (p. 579)

Gunn does not attempt to explain Una's feelings, but by
focusing on her physical reaction he allows the reader to share
them with her.

The novel could end here with Finn's triumphal return and Una's welcome, but as well as suggesting an ending, a coming full circle, Gunn suggests that this sense of an ending is an illusion, that life will carry on, will keep changing, just like the sea.

We end with Finn alone on the eve of his marriage to Una, trying to evade his friends who are intent on putting him through "certain heathenish practices" (p. 582) by way of initiation into this new stage of his life. Determined to outwit them, he seeks refuge at the House of Peace:

> When he was assured that no-one was after him, he performed the mental act of describing the circle of sanctuary around the ground on which he lay. Then his eyes fell on the circle of low flat stones and he crept into its heart. (p. 580)

In the heart of this circle, this symbol of wholeness, Finn feels himself at one with Una and the book ends with this image of Finn and Una in the heart of this circle with life coming for him. He sees himself as a white-haired old man sitting here many years from now. This is the old man of his earlier vision (see p. 214); an image of the wisdom which he has now attained, a wisdom that is fully responsive and alive to life in its living moment, which does not try to refuse or evade life's possibilities, but which remains completely open to them. This kind of awareness is not an end; it is only a beginning:

> What he had lived of life was only its beginning. Its deeper mysteries were ahead. (p. 583)

Notes
1. Highlanders left their doors open in case Christ should appear as a stranger in need of hospitality.

4. CHARACTERS

Fittingly for a novel in which the nature of community is a major theme, the book is rich in characters. The main characters, however, are Tormad, Catrine, Roddie, Kirsty and Finn.

Tormad

Tormad and Catrine are newly-weds at the beginning of the book. With Catrine he seems quiet and shy, but is bold enough to lead the others out to sea in the first attempt at fishing. His shyness can also be seen in the tentativeness with which he sets out to sea, his bravery in the way he challenges the rights of the press-gang who take the men away. Although he is only in the book for the first chapter, his presence is always there in the background for Catrine and for Finn, the son who never knew his father but who shares many of his traits.

Catrine

Eighteen at the beginning of the novel and nearly forty at the end, Catrine is a very impressive character. Like Tormad she is shy, but she also has a fierce, passionate side which she reveals in her attempt to stop him from going to sea. Once widowed she shows great dignity in the way she carries herself in the community, although when we see her with Finn or with Kirsty we see a more relaxed side of her. She selflessly subordinates her own life to the bringing up of her son, and to helping Kirsty run the croft because she feels she owes much to Kirsty for taking her in and giving her a home.

One of Gunn's great successes in his portrayal of Catrine is how he tracks the way she lives her life through Finn and denies other aspects of her personality before showing how she gradually moves beyond this and opens up again to her own sexuality. Although the book is to a large extent Finn's book, Gunn's description of Catrine's inner struggle to grow from a young girl to a mature woman is masterly.

Roddie

Roddie Sinclair is almost an idealised version of the man Tormad might have become. When Catrine meets him he is twenty-five years old and an accomplished fisherman in charge of his own boat and his own crew. He is physically strong but also kind and considerate, although as Finn discovers later, he can be explosively violent when pushed too far. Gunn adds complexity to the character by showing how he changes on marriage to Catrine and on the birth of their first child. The almost excessively "macho" side of his character is toned down as the focus of his life moves from the tough life of the fisherman to the quieter appreciation of domestic happiness. By this point in his life Roddie has no need to prove himself in the eyes of others. That need is picked up by Finn who as a young man starting out in his career feels the need to prove himself very powerfully.

Kirsty
Kirsty MacKay is a wonderfully alive character. Unmarried and helping her widowed father to run his croft she is practical and hard-working. She takes Catrine in and helps her to cope with the loss of Tormad by her uncomplicated and practical response to life. Gunn catches much of this in Kirsty's language. She is not one to hide behind fancy words. Her privileged position as Finn's "granny" allows her to see and comment on the relationship between Catrine and Finn with real insight.

Finn
Not even born at the start of the novel, Finn gradually emerges as its hero. This is quite fitting as he shares a name with Finn MacCoul, one of the great heroes of Celtic literature, a link that is made quite explicit at different points of the story. Yet he is fully realised as a young boy making the difficult transition to adulthood. Parts of the story appear to be told through Finn's eyes, so Gunn re-creates for the reader the world as Finn sees and understands it. Like many of Gunn's characters he seems particularly open to an awareness of the natural world. Living in a pre-modern rural world this is true of most of the characters, but Finn has an eye that notices many details of the world around him and a mind that apprehends their significance. As a fisherman, and as a storyteller that capacity is vital to his success.

His journey to maturity is a traditional subject but Gunn makes it new by the intensity he gives to Finn's struggles, and the complexity and contradiction he reveals in Finn's character. At different times he is loving, adventurous, fearful, proud, angry, bitter, confused, unpleasant. His attitude to others and his treatment of them can be selfish, especially towards the end of the novel when he is struggling to accept his own sexuality and also to accept the fact that his mother as a mature woman in her own right has her own needs and desires. Again, Gunn's treatment of Finn's struggle to become a mature individual separate from his mother who is also a separate individual is one of the strongest features of the novel. The difficulty of his struggle makes it all the more believable.

5. THEMES

The novel is rich in themes. It is a *bildungsroman*, a novel of growing up; it is a novel about the importance of community; about the relationship between the individual and the community; it is about the nature and value of storytelling; it is a novel that explores the movement of history; and it is a novel that explores the tension between traditional ways of living and modern ways of living.

Bildungsroman
The novel follows the development of Finn MacHamish through various rites of passage from birth to the eve of his marriage. His journey towards maturity is one of the most important strands in the narrative. At the same time, Gunn shows Finn's mother Catrine going through her own rites of passage. The relationship between these two characters is explored with great sensitivity and insight.

Traditional versus modern ways of life
In many ways the novel seems to be a hymn to "the old ways". Finn's experiences in the Western Isles where he encounters a more stable and rooted way of life than that which his own background gives him seem to suggest this, and he certainly gains hugely from his time there. Yet Finn himself represents a new way of living in the world. He is more driven, more ambitious than Roddie for instance, and at times he is driven by the idea of making money from his fishing as well as simply enjoying his mastery of the craft. Ultimately he attains a balance between being a valued part of his community and being one of those who help that community to move forward. His deep understanding and appreciation of his culture help him to attain that balance, and that is perhaps one of Gunn's most important messages: in order to survive we need to develop and move on but we should do so by staying connected to an older wisdom.

Storytelling
The novel is itself a supreme example of storytelling, and Finn is a wonderful teller of tales. The ability to engage others

through the power of storytelling whether in prose, poetry or song is one that is highly valued in Scotland because it is a way of teaching people to live creatively, to engage their imagination, in their dealings with the world around them. As well as Highland folk tales and local history and anecdote Gunn also used that wonderful repository of Gaelic lore, *Carmina Gadelica* (edited by Alexander Carmichael) as a source. He had used it in the writing of *Butcher's Broom* and would return to it many times throughout his life. It was important to him not just as a collection of stories, hymns, songs and incantations, but perhaps even more as an example of an attitude or an orientation to the world that was imaginative and creative.

History
For Gunn, official history was often the record left by the victors of any conflict. It was predominantly male, and it generally ignored the lives of ordinary people. One of his aims in *The Silver Darlings* was to redress this imbalance and show how history happens to ordinary people too – often when they feel most ground down by the actions of the rich and powerful. We should not forget that the book was published in 1941, during World War II. Much of Gunn's work during the war years was aimed explicitly at looking for positives during a time of despair. For Douglas Gifford, *Sun Circle, Butcher's Broom* and *The Silver Darlings* form a loose "trilogy" that gives an alternative reading of Scottish history from the clash of paganism with Christianity in the ninth century, through the Highland Clearances of the late eighteenth and early nineteenth centuries to the rise of the fishing industry in the nineteenth century. For Gifford, Gunn offers Scotland a potent myth of regeneration, a renewed sense of how to deal with the tragedy and horror of history and turn it into something vital and sustaining. It is a message that is not only directed at Scotland, but in a century of wars, it was a message for all of mankind.

In exploring the rise of the fishing industry after the trauma of the Highland Clearances, the novel shows an acute awareness of how "history" is not just a record of events but an attempt to understand the way cultures shift and change and develop in response to events. It is a dynamic *process* in which terrible events might eventually have unforeseen but beneficial effects. In time those effects might become less pronounced and the cycle will begin again. Like the sea itself, the movement of history seems vast and unknowable, always coming and going with a seeming inevitability but always startlingly unpredictable.

By the time of *The Grey Coast* the fishing itself was in decline and the Highlands as a region was in need of something else to sustain it. In showing how the prosperity of the fishing industry arose from the poverty and degradation of the Clearances when the landlords moved their people from the land to make room for more profitable sheep, Gunn suggests not so much that history is cyclic but rather that its great movements ebb and flow just like the sea.

The unconscious

Artists have always known about the role of the unconscious in our lives. In the late nineteenth and early twentieth centuries, however, the work of the psychologists Sigmund Freud and Carl Gustav Jung highlighted the role of the unconscious from a more scientific perspective. Gunn was well aware of their work which seemed to resonate with his own instincts as a novelist. In *The Key of the Chest* (1945), he wrote, "Man must for ever move, like a liberator, through his own unconscious" (p. 196). In *The Silver Darlings* the unconscious is everything the characters cannot fully understand about themselves, and the world around them: the sea, sexuality, motherhood, widowhood, love. Part of the book's success is the subtlety with which Gunn explores his characters' attempts to grasp the totality of their lives, conscious and unconscious together in a creative balance.

6. STYLE AND LANGUAGE

The Silver Darlings is a big novel. Douglas Gifford describes it as "symphonic" in scope and in structure because of the way it introduces, develops and extends motifs and symbols throughout its length. J. B. Pick calls it Tolstoyan, because it echoes the way the great nineteenth century Russian novelist allowed the reader to focus on many different characters and locations while keeping the main narrative moving.

Another way to consider the structure and style of the book would be to see it as a Celtic knot with themes and characters intertwined and echoing each other over time. This allows Gunn to describe his characters' development as individuals while simultaneously allowing them to take on archetypal significance. Tormad, Roddie and Finn, for instance, could all be seen as variants of the archetypal hero figure. Tormad's quest ends in disaster, Finn's in success. Roddie, interestingly as the older man, is so successful in his quest that he is able to move beyond it and live a different sort of life, becoming a different sort of hero. In this he is like James Joyce's Leopold Bloom, the "hero" of his novel *Ulysses*, an ordinary man trying his best to live a decent life in a world that seems inimical to this.

Finn's mother, Catrine, too, has something of this dual characterisation about her. She is a young woman of spirit who has to deal with the early loss of her husband and survive to bring up her son in a harsh world. She is wife, widow and mother and has to learn to take on these roles in her community and in herself. It is not easy and in a country whose novels are often dominated by strong male characters, Gunn's achievement in putting such a strong female character at the heart of his novel should be applauded. His portrayal of Kirsty McKay is also a moving description of a certain kind of older Scottish woman who may not exist any longer in our changing social patterns but certainly existed in Scotland up until the very recent past: practical, witty and caring but with a sharp tongue in her head.

The Silver Darlings is written in English, but we are constantly reminded that most of the main characters would be speaking in Gaelic, so the rhythms and speech patterns of that language are echoed. Gunn himself was not a Gaelic speaker but his father spoke Gaelic to his crew when at sea, so his attempt to recreate the speech of his characters has some personal authority. Several of the descriptions of the sea and of some of the boats seem also to owe something to similar descriptions in Gaelic poetry which he would know from translations.

One of the features that gives Gunn's language its particular "tang" is the way he moves easily between the elusive language of abstract thought and the concrete language of physical description.

7. CONCLUSION

The Silver Darlings is a novel about a particular moment in Scottish history. It explores the aftermath of the Highland Clearances in the early nineteenth century, and shows how the people of a particular place overcame the hardship and horror of being moved from the land by their landlords. They did this by building up the fishing industry, and so became part of a larger European move towards the various forms of industrialisation that have largely shaped our own world.

As a historical novel, the book builds on Walter Scott's explorations of particular moments in Scottish history. Like Scott, too, Gunn writes about these moments in such a way as to suggest continuities and parallels that make the past seem to be still alive in our speech and in our social attitudes. Gunn does not want Scotland to go back to some imagined rural "golden age". Instead, he wants us to move forward, to change and develop in our personal lives and in our communities, without losing what was best in the past.

More importantly, the general thrust of his work is to make us examine the way we live as individuals and as a society in order to develop a way of living that is sane and sustainable. *The Silver Darlings* was written and published in a dark time of war and is a heartening exploration of how, faced with such darkness, we can still move towards the light.

8. BIBLIOGRAPHY

Major works by Neil M. Gunn

The Grey Coast, London: Jonathan Cape, 1926.

Hidden Doors [Stories], Edinburgh: The Porpoise Press, 1929.

Morning Tide, Edinburgh: The Porpoise Press, 1930.

The Lost Glen, Edinburgh: The Porpoise Press, 1932.

Sun Circle, Edinburgh: The Porpoise Press, 1933.

Butcher's Broom. Edinburgh: The Porpoise Press, 1934.

Whisky and Scotland: A Practical and Spiritual Guide, London: Routledge, 1935.

Highland River, Edinburgh: The Porpoise Press, 1937.

Off in a Boat [Travel], London: Faber & Faber, 1938.

Wild Geese Overhead, London: Faber & Faber, 1939.

Second Sight, London: Faber & Faber, 1940.

The Silver Darlings, London: Faber & Faber, 1941.

Young Art and Old Hector, London: Faber & Faber, 1942.

Storm and Precipice [Selected extracts], London: Faber & Faber, 1942.

The Serpent, London: Faber & Faber, 1943.

The Green Isle of the Great Deep, London: Faber & Faber, 1944.

The Key of the Chest, London: Faber & Faber, 1945.

The Drinking Well, London: Faber & Faber, 1946.

The Shadow, London: Faber & Faber, 1948.

The Silver Bough, London: Faber & Faber, 1948.

The Lost Chart, London: Faber & Faber, 1949.

Highland Pack [Essays], London: Faber & Faber, 1949.

The White Hour and Other Stories, London: Faber & Faber, 1950.

The Well at the World's End, London: Faber & Faber, 1951.

Bloodhunt, London: Faber & Faber, 1952.

The Other Landscape, London: Faber & Faber, 1954.

The Atom of Delight [Autobiographical], London: Faber & Faber, 1956.

Works published posthumously

Neil M. Gunn: Selected Letters [ed. J. B. Pick],
Edinburgh: Polygon, 1987.

Landscape to Light [Essays, ed. Alistair McCleery and
Dairmid Gunn], Dunbeath: Whittles Publishing, 2009.

Half-Light and Other Short Stories [ed Dairmid Gunn],
Dunbeath: Whittles Publishing, 2011

Belief in Ourselves [Essays, ed. Alistair McCleery and
Dairmid Gunn], Dunbeath, Whittles Publishing, 2012.

Books about Neil Gunn

Burns, J., *A Celebration of the Light: Zen in the Novels of
Neil Gunn*, Edinburgh: Canongate, 1988.

Gifford, D., *Neil M. Gunn and Lewis Grassic Gibbon*,
Edinburgh: Oliver and Boyd, 1983.

Gunn, D. and Murray, I. (eds.), *Neil Gunn's Country:
Essays in Celebration of Neil Gunn*, Edinburgh:
Chambers, 1991.

Hart, F. R. and Pick, J. B., *Neil M. Gunn: A Highland
Life*, London: John Murray, 1981.

Morrison, D. (ed.), *Essays on Neil Gunn*, Thurso:
Humphries, 1971.

Palmer McCulloch, M., *The Novels of Neil M. Gunn: A
Critical Study*, Edinburgh: Scottish Academic Press,
1987.

Pick, J. B., *Neil M. Gunn*, Northcote House in association
with the British Council, 2004.

Price, R., *The Fabulous Matter of Fact: The Poetics of
Neil M. Gunn*, Edinburgh: Edinburgh University
Press, 1991.

Scott, A. and Gifford, D., *Neil M. Gunn: The Man and the
Writer*, Edinburgh: Blackwood, 1973.

Stokoe, C. J. L., *A Bibliography of the Works of Neil M.
Gunn*, Aberdeen: Aberdeen University Press, 1987.

Lightning Source UK Ltd.
Milton Keynes UK
UKHW021848030221
378186UK00007B/292

9 781906 841188